Award-Winning
CHESS
PROBLEMS

Burt Hochberg

**PUZZLE
WRIGHT
PRESS**

An imprint of Sterling
Publishing Co., Inc.

www.puzzlewright.com

Also by Burt Hochberg

Title Chess: The 1972 U.S. Chess Championship

Winning With Chess Psychology (with Pal Benko)

The 64-Square Looking Glass: The Great Game of Chess in World Literature

Chess Braintwisters

Sit & Solve Chess Problems

Mensa Guide to Chess: 30 Days to Great Chess

Puzzlewright Press and the distinctive Puzzlewright Press logo are registered trademarks of Sterling Publishing Co., Inc.

Library of Congress Cataloging-in-Publication Data
Hochberg, Burt.
Award-winning chess problems / Burt Hochberg.
   p. cm.—(Official Mensa puzzle book)
Includes index.
ISBN 1-4027-1145-X
1. Chess problems. I. Title: Chess problems. II. Title. III. Series.

GV1451.H615 2005
794.1'2—dc22

2004066244

6   8   10   9   7   5

Published by Sterling Publishing Co., Inc.
387 Park Avenue South, New York, NY 10016
© 2005 by Burt Hochberg
Distributed in Canada by Sterling Publishing
C/o Canadian Manda Group, 165 Dufferin Street
Toronto, Ontario, Canada M6K 3H6
Distributed in the United Kingdom by GMC Distribution Services
Castle Place, 166 High Street, Lewes, East Sussex, England BN7 1XU
Distributed in Australia by Capricorn Link (Australia) Pty. Ltd.
P.O. Box 704, Windsor, NSW 2756, Australia

Manufactured in the United States of America
All rights reserved

Sterling ISBN 978-1-4027-1145-9

For information about custom editions, special sales, premium and
corporate purchases, please contact Sterling Special Sales
Department at 800-805-5489 or specialsales@sterlingpublishing.com.

CONTENTS

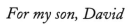

For my son, David

INTRODUCTION

Each of these problems has been awarded a top prize in one of the innumerable problem competitions (tourneys) that have been held all over the world in the last century and a half. Problem composers submit their works to committees whose members comprise other composers, problem judges, and problem magazine editors. These experts determine the prizewinners in several categories.

Advanced solvers will no doubt recognize the various "themes" that constructors like to use such as the Nowotny Interference, the Wurzburg-Plachutta, the Dual Avoidance, the Rukhlis, the Stocchi, and other exotic birds. Since this book is not intended primarily for the advanced solver (although many of the problems here are challenging enough for them), I have decided to ignore all talk of themes and have chosen problems that inexperienced solvers, without knowing anything about themes, should be able to solve through diligent and I hope pleasurable effort.

All orthodox chess problems, like those in this book, stipulate that White makes the first move (the key) and checkmates Black in a specified number of moves no matter what Black plays. The stipulation is inviolable: mate must be accomplished in exactly the number of moves specified, no more, no fewer. There is only one correct key for each problem.

All the problems in this book are orthodox two-move direct mates, which simply means that they are not helpmates, self-mates, maximummers, retroselfstalemates, or other unorthodox forms. The stipulation for a two-mover is that White is to move first and mate on his second move no matter how Black tries to defend. Black will be unsuccessful, of course. As solver, your task is to find the key that unlocks the puzzle and then to work out the ensuing mate after every possible Black response.

In a two-mover, White's first move sets up the mate in one of two ways. White either directly threatens a specific mate on the next move (a "threat-problem") or plays a waiting move that threatens nothing but waits for Black to make a move that allows mate. Knowing what type of position a problem is should be a helpful first step in solving it: if the position is mostly blocked, with almost no pawn moves and few piece moves for Black, then White's first move is most likely a waiting move; this is a "block-problem" or a "zugzwang" position. Zugzwang is a very important stratagem not only in problems but also in ordinary chess play. It's a German word that means "compulsion to move." A player in zugzwang is required to move, thereby weakening his position or losing the game outright.

Another helpful clue is that none of the problems in this book has a checking key.

If you have trouble finding a solution despite your best efforts (don't give up without a fight!), you may avail yourself of a hint. But be warned: though most hints are instantly helpful, some are cryptic and require a little extra thinking.

For their invaluable help in preparing this book, I'm grateful to my amazing wife, Carol, and my extraordinary editor, Peter Gordon.

1. V. Diaconu, Der Waarheid 1967

White to move and mate in two
Hint, page 70

2. J. Dobrescu, Shakhmaty v SSSR 1956

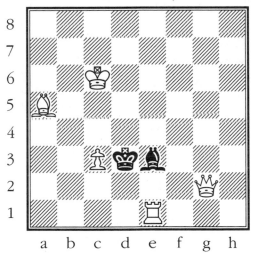

White to move and mate in two
Hint, page 71

3. F. Gamage, Chess Correspondent 1941

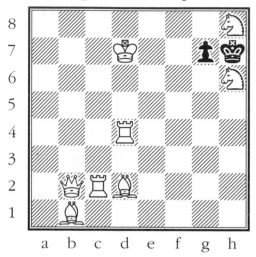

White to move and mate in two
Hint, page 72

4. E. Kahane, Salut Public 1929

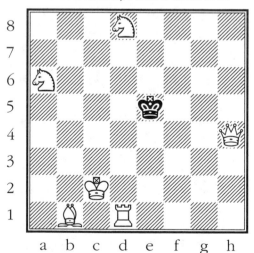

White to move and mate in two
Hint, page 73

5. H. des Marands amd P. Monreal, La Marseillaise 1945

White to move and mate in two
Hint, page 70

6. O. Wurzburg, Pittsburgh Gazette Times 1917

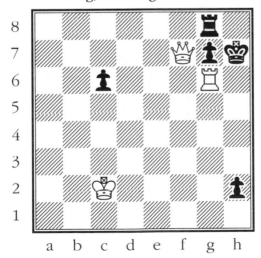

White to move and mate in two
Hint, page 71

7. M. Caillaud, Probleemblad 1985

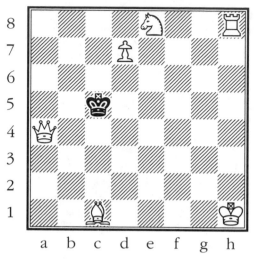

White to move and mate in two
Hint, page 72

8. M. Kovacevich, D. Ljubomirovich, Mat Plus 1996

White to move and mate in two
Hint, page 73

9. M. Marandjuk, Smena 1993

White to move and mate in two

Hint, page 70

10. M. Musil, Sahmatny zurnal 1892

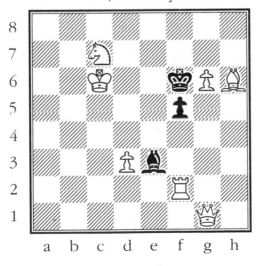

White to move and mate in two

Hint, page 71

11. W.A. Shinkman, Huddlesfield College Magazine 1887

White to move and mate in two
Hint, page 72

12. W.B. Rice, Good Companions 1915

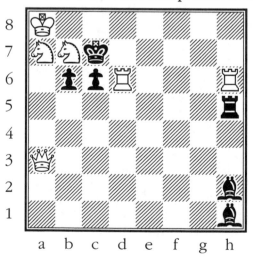

White to move and mate in two
Hint, page 73

13. A. Galitsky, Shakhmatnoye obozreniye 1892

White to move and mate in two
Hint, page 70

14. O. Wurzburg, Gazette, Times 1917

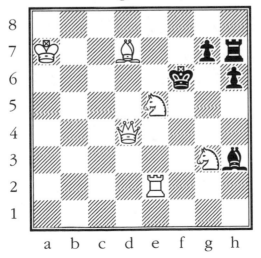

White to move and mate in two
Hint, page 71

15. L. Kubbel, Deutsche Schachzeitung 1909

White to move and mate in two
Hint, page 72

16. T. Vesz, Good Companions 1923

White to move and mate in two
Hint, page 73

17. J. Vakuska, Sahove umenie 1994

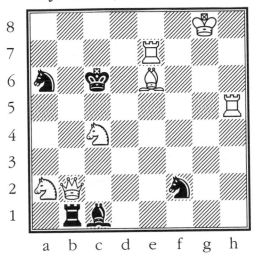

White to move and mate in two

Hint, page 70

18. H. Tuxen, Good Companions 1922

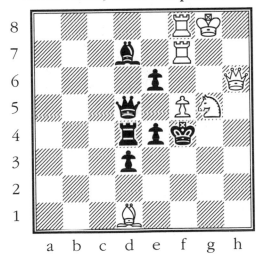

White to move and mate in two

Hint, page 71

19. H.H. Tucker, Melbourne Times 1919

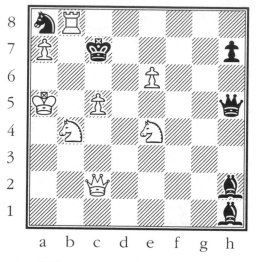

White to move and mate in two
Hint, page 72

20. A.G. Stubbs, Hampstead Express 1914

White to move and mate in two
Hint, page 73

21. A.G. Stubbs, Good Companions 1918

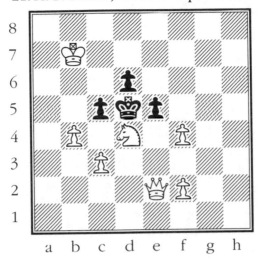

White to move and mate in two
Hint, page 70

22. L.B. Salkind, Die Schwalbe 1912

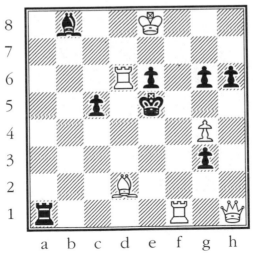

White to move and mate in two
Hint, page 71

23. B.G. Laws, Northern Figaro 1888

a b c d e f g h

White to move and mate in two
Hint, page 72

24. V. Marin, Sydney Herald 1898

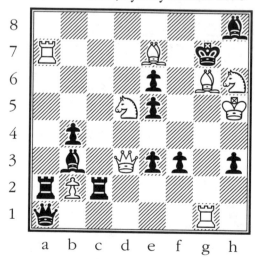

a b c d e f g h

White to move and mate in two
Hint, page 73

25. A. Mari, La Scacchista 1921

White to move and mate in two
Hint, page 70

26. M. Lipton, British Chess Problem Society 1986

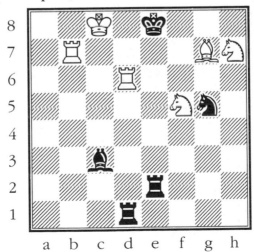

White to move and mate in two
Hint, page 71

27. A.F. Kallaway, Football Field 1904

White to move and mate in two
Hint, page 72

28. G. Heathcote, Revue d'Echecs 1904

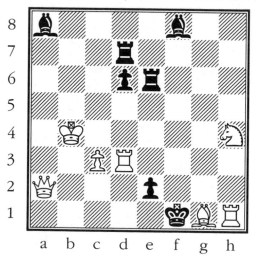

White to move and mate in two
Hint, page 73

29. K. Hannemann, Brisbane Courier 1920

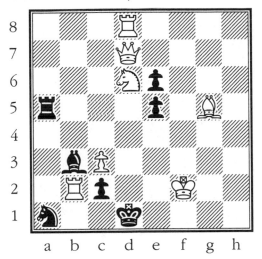

White to move and mate in two

Hint, page 70

30. G. Guidelli, Good Companions 1918

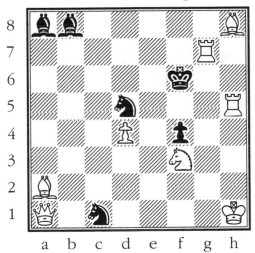

White to move and mate in two

Hint, page 71

31. M. Grunfeld, Münchener Post 1937

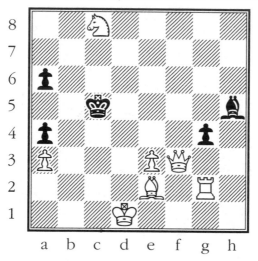

White to move and mate in two

Hint, page 72

32. A.G. Fellows, Birmingham Mercury 1895

White to move and mate in two

Hint, page 73

33. O. Stocchi, Ajedrez Español 1952

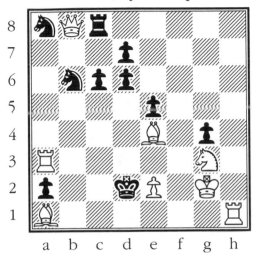

White to move and mate in two
Hint, page 70

34. J.J. O'Keefe, Melbourne Leader 1909

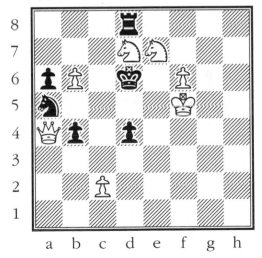

White to move and mate in two
Hint, page 71

35. F.A.L. Kuskop, Otago Witness 1898

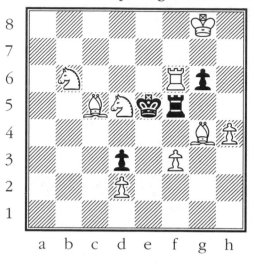

White to move and mate in two
Hint, page 72

36. G. Hume, British Chess Magazine 1933

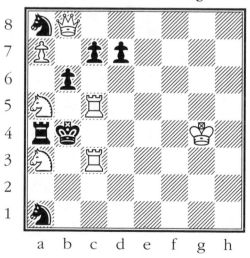

White to move and mate in two
Hint, page 73

37. H. Cudmore, Hackney Mercury 1902

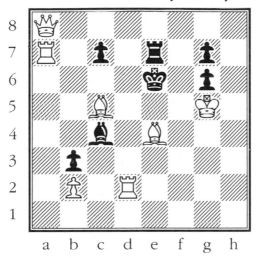

White to move and mate in two
Hint, page 70

38. V. Chepizny, 64 1980

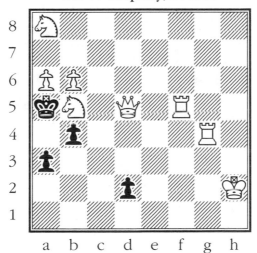

White to move and mate in two
Hint, page 71

39. H.W. Bettmann, Good Companions 1924

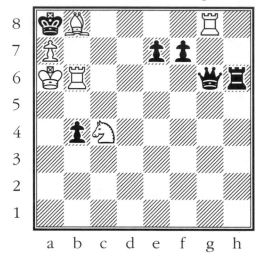

White to move and mate in two
Hint, page 72

40. J. Beszczynski, Start 1955-56

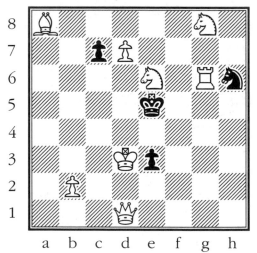

White to move and mate in two
Hint, page 73

41. H.W. Sherrard, Sheffield Independent 1886

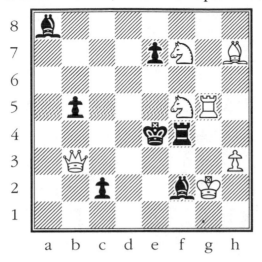

White to move and mate in two
Hint, page 70

42. G. Heathcote, American Chess Bulletin 1911

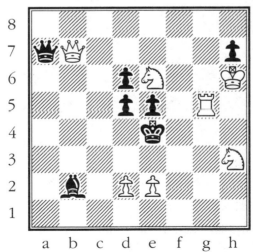

White to move and mate in two
Hint, page 71

43. A. Ellerman, Alfiere di Re 1922

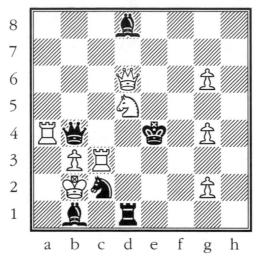

White to move and mate in two
Hint, page 72

44. V.F. Rudenko, Cervonij girnik 1975

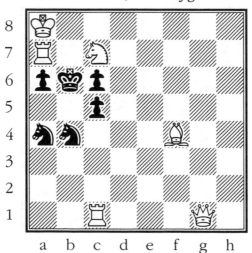

White to move and mate in two
Hint, page 73

45. A. Bottacchi, Brisbane Courier 1919

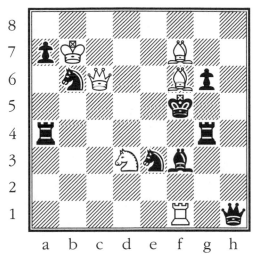

White to move and mate in two
Hint, page 70

46. H.W. Barry, La Stratégie 1901

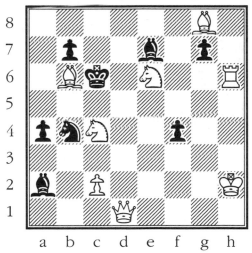

White to move and mate in two
Hint, page 71

47. M. Feigl, Tijdskrift 1904

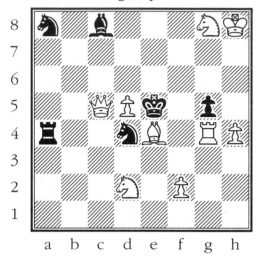

White to move and mate in two
Hint, page 72

48. A.G. Stubbs, Good Companions 1920

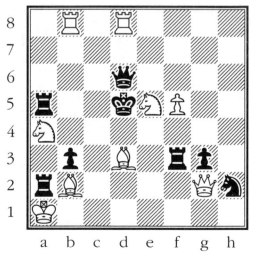

White to move and mate in two
Hint, page 73

49. K. Grabowski, Tygodnik 1913

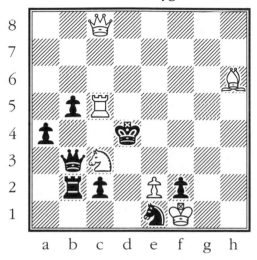

White to move and mate in two
Hint, page 70

50. H.E. Funk, Good Companions 1923

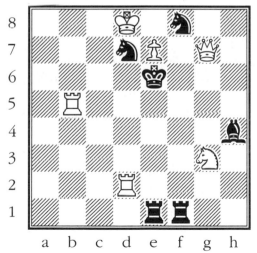

White to move and mate in two
Hint, page 71

51. G. Heathcote, Healey Memorial Tourney 1901

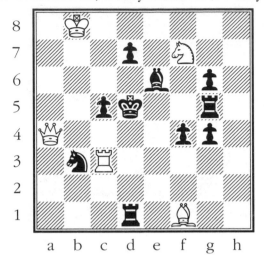

White to move and mate in two
Hint, page 72

52. J.C. Wainwright, Good Companions 1914

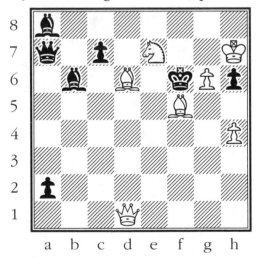

White to move and mate in two
Hint, page 73

53. J. van Dyke, Tijdschrift 1903

White to move and mate in two
Hint, page 70

54. A. van der Ven, Tijdschrift 1912

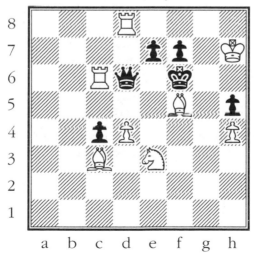

White to move and mate in two
Hint, page 71

55. B. Djakuk, Diagrammes 1994

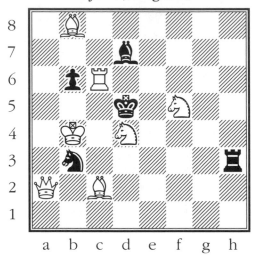

a b c d e f g h

White to move and mate in two

Hint, page 72

56. L.K. A. Kubbel, Tijdskrift 1917

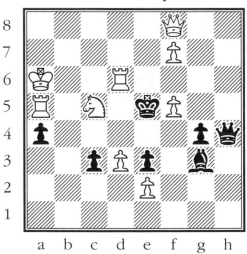

a b c d e f g h

White to move and mate in two

Hint, page 73

57. G. Guidelli, La Scacchiera 1920

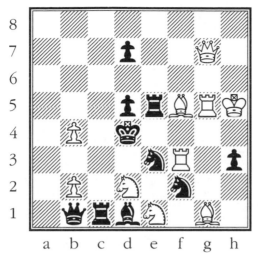

White to move and mate in two
Hint, page 70

58. C.A. Gilberg, Danbury News 1881

White to move and mate in two
Hint, page 71

59. Z. Kolodnas, L'Echiquier de Paris 1927

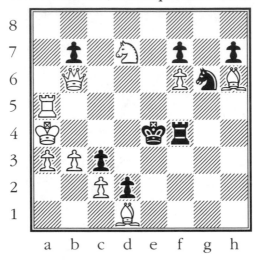

White to move and mate in two
Hint, page 72

60. C.W. Sheppard, Good Companions 1921

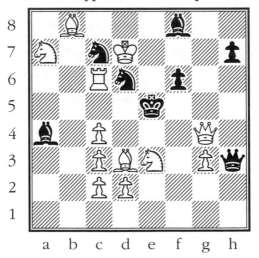

White to move and mate in two
Hint, page 73

61. P.F. Blake, Football Field 1902

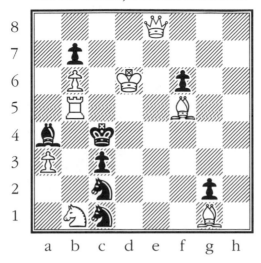

White to move and mate in two
Hint, page 70

62. H.W. Bettmann, Southern Trade Gazette 1895

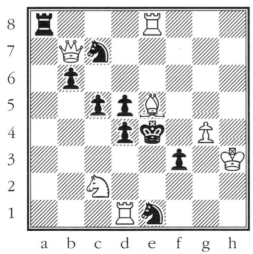

White to move and mate in two
Hint, page 71

63. J. Opdenoordt, Tijdschrift 1917

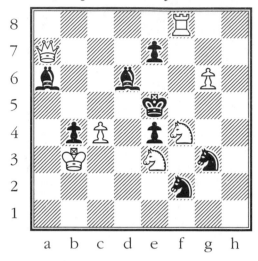

White to move and mate in two
Hint, page 72

64. J.J. O'Keefe, Brisbane Courier 1916

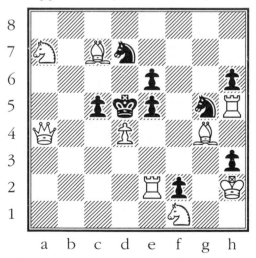

White to move and mate in two
Hint, page 73

65. V. Marin, Spanish National Tourney 1919

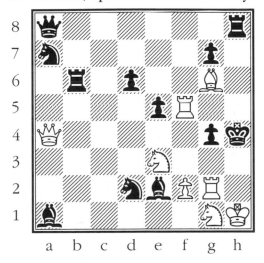

White to move and mate in two
Hint, page 70

66. L. Loshinski & L. Zagoruiko, Sport Kommittee USSR 1950

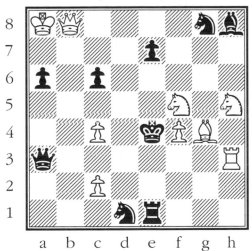

White to move and mate in two
Hint, page 71

67. J.K. Heydon, Good Companions 1920

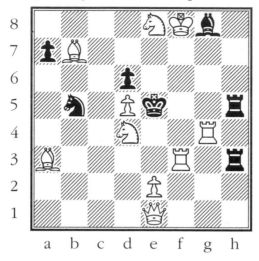

White to move and mate in two
Hint, page 72

68. E. Pape, Good Companions, April 1923

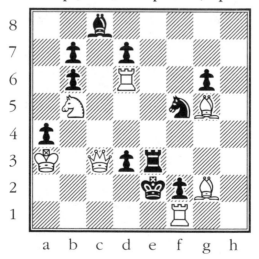

White to move and mate in two
Hint, page 73

69. C. Mansfield, Densmore Memorial 1918-20

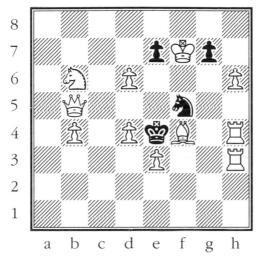

White to move and mate in two
Hint, page 70

70. C. Mansfield, Good Companions 1917

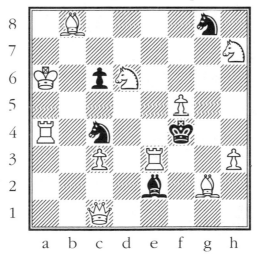

White to move and mate in two
Hint, page 71

71. K.A.K. Larsen, Revista Argentina 1920

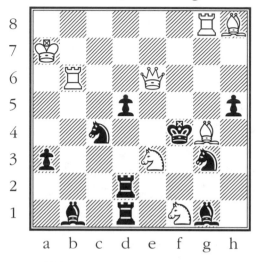

White to move and mate in two
Hint, page 72

72. F.A.L. Kuskop, Canterbury Times 1900-01

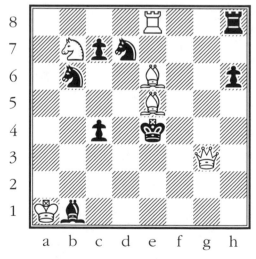

White to move and mate in two
Hint, page 73

73. E. Rukhlis, Concours de Sverdlovsk 1946

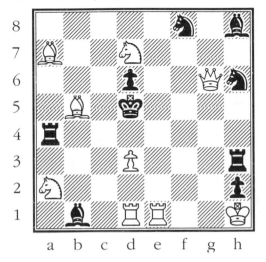

White to move and mate in two
Hint, page 70

74. G. Guidelli, Brisbane Courier 1918

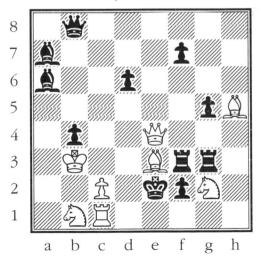

White to move and mate in two
Hint, page 71

75. K. Grabowski, Haagsche Post 1921

White to move and mate in two

Hint, page 72

76. F. Gamage, British Chess Magazine Theme Tourney 1944

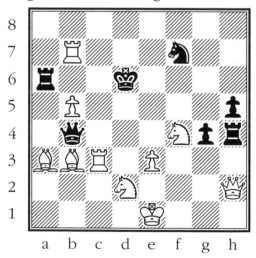

White to move and mate in two

Hint, page 73

77. F. Gamage, Tidskrift 1914

White to move and mate in two
Hint, page 70

78. D.W.A. Brotherton, McWilliam Tourney 1955

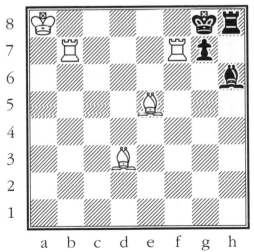

White to move and mate in two
Hint, page 71

79. M. de Moraes, Football Field 1913

White to move and mate in two
Hint, page 72

80. D. Kanonik, Lokker Memorial Tourney 1975

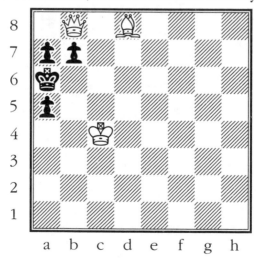

White to move and mate in two
Hint, page 73

81. A. Ellerman, L'Italia Scacchistica 1951

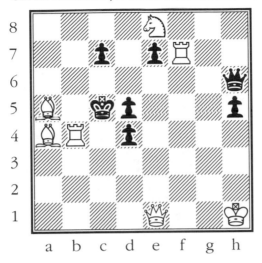

White to move and mate in two
Hint, page 70

82. P. Feenstra Kuiper, Good Companions 1916

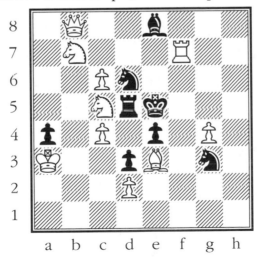

White to move and mate in two
Hint, page 71

83. P.F. Blake, Western Daily Mercury 1906

White to move and mate in two
Hint, page 72

84. F.B. Feast, Good Companions 1924

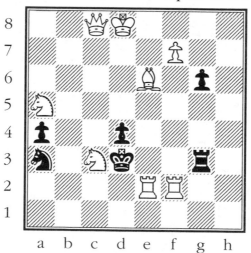

White to move and mate in two
Hint, page 73

85. A.W. Daniel, Western Daily Mercury 1911

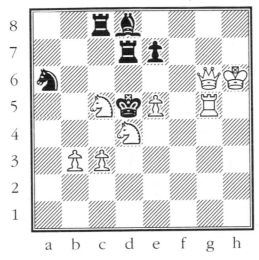

White to move and mate in two

Hint, page 70

86. A. Bottacchi, Illustrazione Italiana 1921

White to move and mate in two

Hint, page 71

87. A. Bottacchi, Densmore Memorial 1918-20

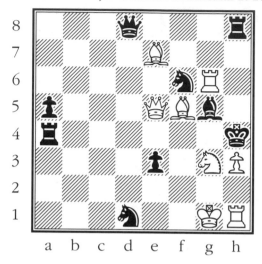

White to move and mate in two
Hint, page 72

88. M. Barulin, Il Problema 1944

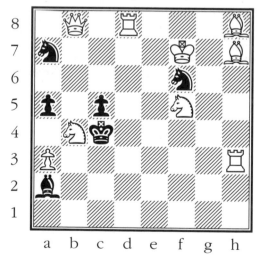

White to move and mate in two
Hint, page 73

89. G.C. Alvey, Hampshire Post 1920

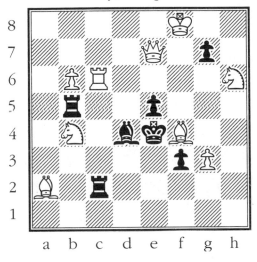

White to move and mate in two
Hint, page 70

90. W.B. Rice, Good Companions 1918

White to move and mate in two
Hint, page 71

91. M. Niemeijer, Jan Hartong, H. Prins, De Waarheid 1985

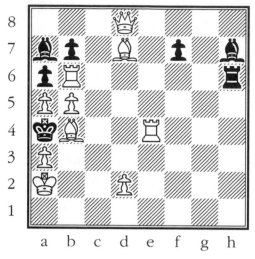

White to move and mate in two
Hint, page 72

92. A.F. Mackenzie, Brighton Society 1901

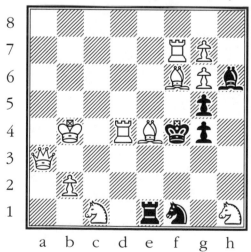

White to move and mate in two
Hint, page 73

93. Kraemer, Kockelkorn Memorial Tourney 1921

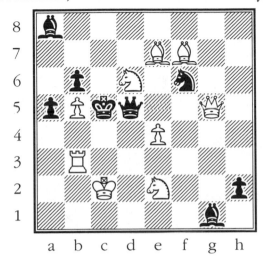

White to move and mate in two
Hint, page 70

94. A. Ianovic, Revista Romana de Sah 1933

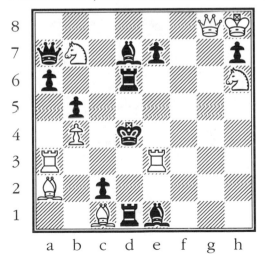

White to move and mate in two
Hint, page 71

95. J.K. Heydon, Australian Columns 1921

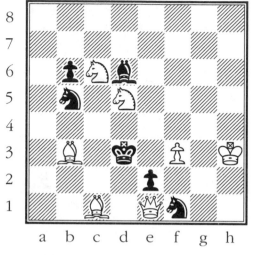

White to move and mate in two
Hint, page 72

96. C.G. Gavrilov, Tidskrift 1907

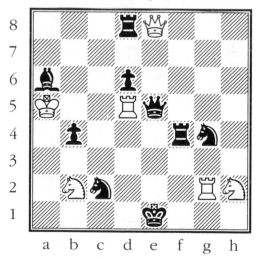

White to move and mate in two
Hint, page 73

97. A. Ellerman, Good Companions 1919

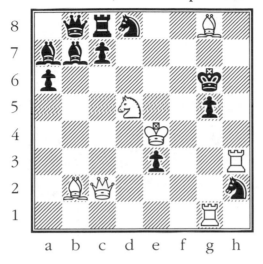

White to move and mate in two
Hint, page 70

98. R.G. Thomson, Norwich Mercury 1902-03

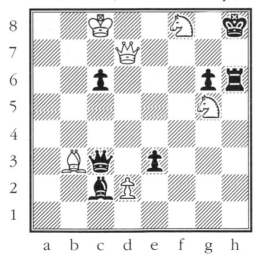

White to move and mate in two
Hint, page 71

99. G. Guidelli, Good Companions 1917

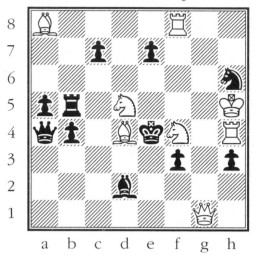

White to move and mate in two
Hint, page 72

100. A. Bottacchi, Hampshire Post 1920

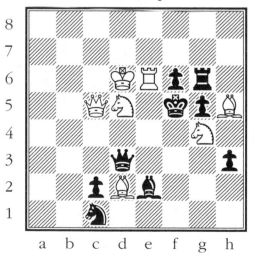

White to move and mate in two
Hint, page 73

101. K.A. Larsen, Good Companions 1920

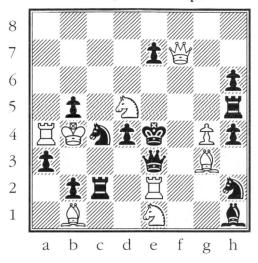

White to move and mate in two
Hint, page 70

102. L. Loshinsky, Abastumansky Shakhmaty Bureau

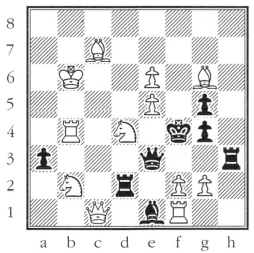

White to move and mate in two
Hint, page 71

103. J.D. Williams, Hampstead and Highgate Express 1907

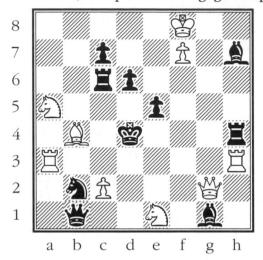

White to move and mate in two
Hint, page 72

104. M. Velimirovic, Mat Plus 1997

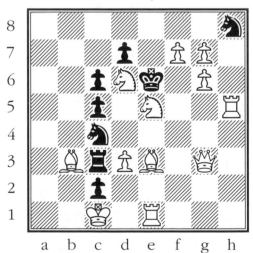

White to move and mate in two
Hint, page 73

105. C. Mansfield, La Settimana Enigmastica 1935

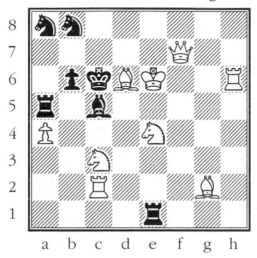

White to move and mate in two

Hint, page 70

106. C. Mansfield, El Ajedrez Argentino 1921

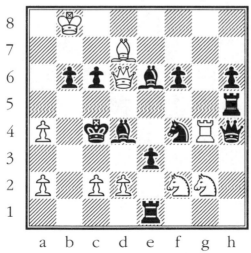

White to move and mate in two

Hint, page 71

107. F. Libby, Morning Post 1901

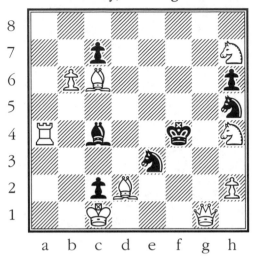

White to move and mate in two
Hint, page 72

108. W. Langstaff, Kent County Congress 1921

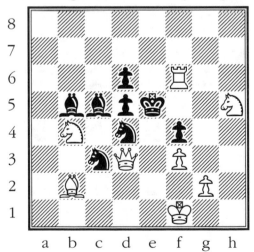

White to move and mate in two
Hint, page 73

109. A.J. Fink, Los Angeles Examiner 1919

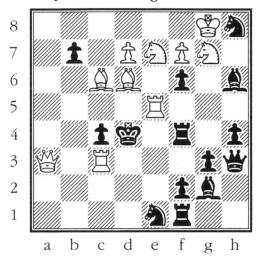

White to move and mate in two
Hint, page 70

110. A. Ellerman, Brisbane Courier 1919

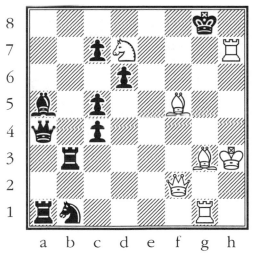

White to move and mate in two
Hint, page 71

111. A. Ellerman, Good Companions 1916

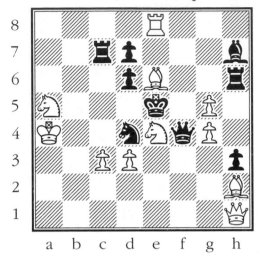

White to move and mate in two
Hint, page 72

112. W.A. Clank, Hackney Mercury 1895

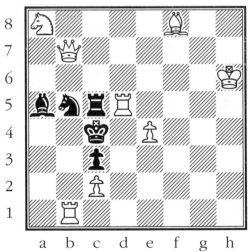

White to move and mate in two
Hint, page 73

113. D. Booth, Good Companions 1915

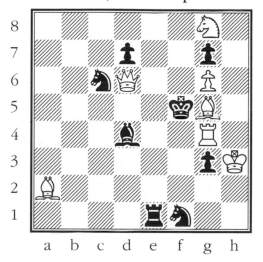

White to move and mate in two
Hint, page 70

114. P.F. Blake, London Observer 1920

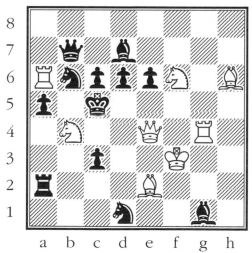

White to move and mate in two
Hint, page 71

115. P.F. Blake, Hampstead Express 1911

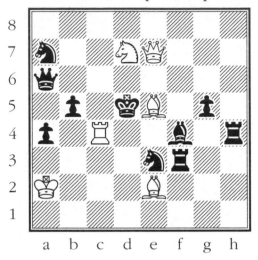

White to move and mate in two
Hint, page 72

116. P.F. Blake, Football Field 1904

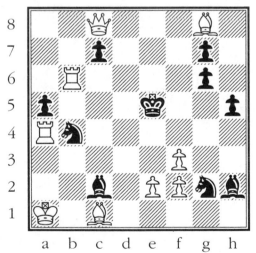

White to move and mate in two
Hint, page 73

117. G.F. Anderson (after H. Weenink), B.C.P.S. 1918

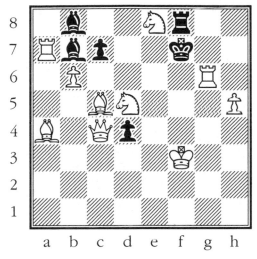

White to move and mate in two

Hint, page 70

118. F. Schrüfer, Nuova Revista 1876

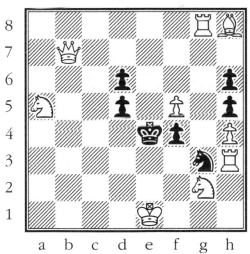

White to move and mate in two

Hint, page 71

119. E. Puig y Puig, Spanish National Tourney 1920

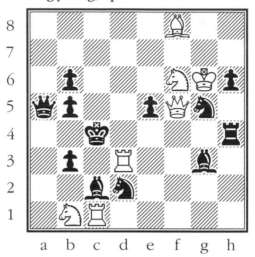

White to move and mate in two
Hint, page 72

120. H. Prins, Wola Gulowska 1992

White to move and mate in two
Hint, page 73

121. A. Piatesi, Parallèles 50, 1948

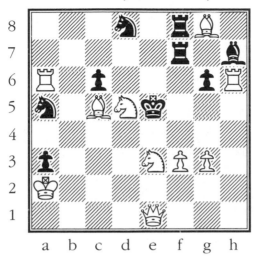

White to move and mate in two
Hint, page 70

122. L.S. Penrose, London Observer 1921

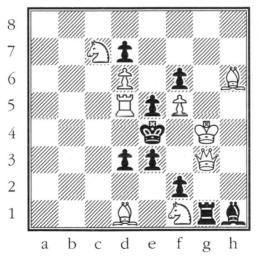

White to move and mate in two
Hint, page 71

67

123. L. Loshinski, Sahs (Riga) 1962

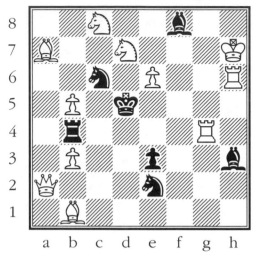

White to move and mate in two
Hint, page 72

124. P.F. Blake, Hampstead Express 1904

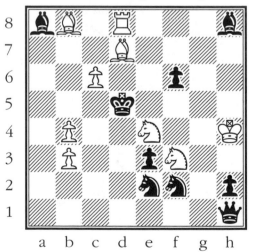

White to move and mate in two
Hint, page 73

125. G. Heathcote, Norwich Mercury 1907

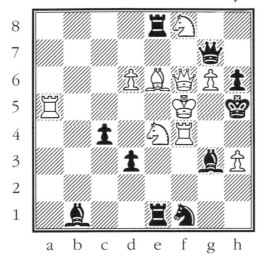

White to move and mate in two

Hint, page 70

THE HINTS

The hints are given in four lists so that while peeking at one hint you won't inadvertently see the next one in sequence. Admittedly, this makes it a little harder to find specific hints, but maybe you won't need them at all. Some hints should make solving particular problems easier; other are somewhat cryptic and may do just the opposite.

1. The queen gets around.
5. The queen needs air.
9. Rook moves.
13. Make no threat
17. A rook goes west.
21. Itty-bitty non-threat.
25. Block the king.
29. A big queen triangle.
33. The queen is in a cage.
37. Rook moves.
41. Rook moves.
45. The bishops have their fun.
49. Rook moves.
53. The knight's triple play.
57. A bishop does not go to h7.
61. The queen is the key.
65. The queen sticks to a diagonal.
69. You like triangles?
73. A little modesty is in order.
77. Abandon ye not the Rd5.
81. A brave knight.
85. Somewhere down the line, expect a pawn discovery.
89. Set up a neat discovery.
93. The queen hides.
97. A long-distance runner.
101. The Nd5 is hanging.
105. The king threatens.
109. A small triangle.
113. Home again.
117. Out of the frying pan, into the fire?
121. The mighty queen shows its stuff.
125. Self-pin and discovery.

3. Rook moves, but which one?
7. One more knight.
11. A counterintuitive bishop move.
15. The threat is 2. Qh1#.
19. A knight two-step.
23. Checks abound, but the key isn't one of them.
27. The pawn can wait.
31. Ruy Lopez?
35. Which knight moves where?
39. A bishop discovery is answered by 1. ... Qxg8.
43. Keep the Black queen pinned.
47. Queen switches sides.
51. Rook moves.
55. Trade a pin for a discovery.
59. Why block the queen?
63. The square g8 beckons.
67. Keep the d-pawn protected.
71. The rook tells the queen, "cuddle up a little closer."
75. Another triangle.
79. Break the knot.
83. What if the rook were not pinned?
87. Get thee hence, bishop!
91. Rook moves.
95. Promotion does not help Black.
99. Give the lady a seat.
103. Ye olde English.
107. The Black bishop gets a taste of freedom.
111. Knight moves.
115. Keep your eye on the Black rooks.
119. It's a good thing the bishop on c2 is pinned.
123. The key threatens mate on the c-file.

THE SOLUTIONS

The first move of a problem solution is called the key. All relevant defenses by Black are given; that is, those that attempt to meet the threat presented by the key. Some keys are not threats at all but waiting moves. Such positions are zugzwang problems, where any Black move is fatal and allows White to mate on the next move.

Moves by the same piece to different squares are bunched together but separated by slashes; for instance, 1. ... Nf8/h8/e5/h4, which is an abbreviated way or writing 1. ...Nf8, 1. ... Nh8, 1. ... Ne8, 1. ... Nh4.

The symbol ~ means "any," "+" means check, and "#" is checkmate.

1. The very mobile queen seems to threaten various mates, such as after 1. Qf4. But 1. ... f1=Q stops them; e.g., 2. Rh8+ Qh3. And 1. Qb1 doesn't work because of 1. ... Kh2. The key is 1. Qb2!. If now 1. ... f1=Q or B, 2. Ng3#, if 1. ... f1=R, then 2. Ng3# or 2. Qg2#, and if 1. ... f1=N 2. Qg2#. If 1. ... Kh2, the queen demonstrates its range with 2. Qh8#.

2. Notwithstanding all those powerful White pieces surrounding the Black king, the correct key is the little move 1. c4. On any bishop reply, 2. Qe4 is mate (except 1. ...Bd4 2. Qe2#). If 1. ...Kxc4 or 1. ... Kd4, then 2. Qd5# does it. The try 1. Kd5?, threatening 2. Qe2#, fails, however, to 1. ... Bf2. With White's bishop not controlling d2, the king finds shelter at d2.

3. The key is not a check, a move usually considered "too strong" and "inelegant" (although some problems do have a checking key). That rules out any move by the Rc2. But 1. Rf4 sets up some interesting mates. If 1. ... gxh6 or 1. ... Kxh8 2. Rc8#. If 1. ... g6 2. Rf7#. If 1. ... g5 2. Rc6#. If 1. ... Kxh6 2. Rh4#.

4. The surprising key, 1. Kd3!, blocks White's own rook and bishop but leaves Black in zugzwang. If 1. ... Kd6 2. Ke4. If 1. ... Kd5 2. Qd4#. Finally, if 1. ... Kf5, White's king continues its murderous march with 2. Kd4#.

5. The key, 1. Nh4, frees the queen and threatens 2. Qf3#. If 1. ... Kf1 2. Rf4#. If 1. ... Kg3 2. Qxg1#. If 1. ... Bh2 2. Qe1#.

6. Not a difficult problem but a very appealing one from a true grandmaster of chess composition, Otto Wurzburg. Black is threatening to queen his h-pawn and make all sorts of trouble. White can't allow that, and he must also maintain his own mating threat on g7. Nothing is gained by moving the queen or king, and the rook must stay on the g-file. The logical key is therefore 1. Rg1!. If 1. ... fxg1=Q 2. Qh5#, or 1. ... h1=Q 2. Rxh1#. Any other rook move allows the pawn to queen, and there goes the mate.

7. Solus rex—the lone king—is a monarch stripped of its defenders and naked to its enemies. Yet White, although he possesses a queen, a rook, a knight, and a bishop, does not have quite enough to force to mate in two. He needs one more piece: 1. d8=N! solves the problem. If 1. ... Kd5 2 Rh5#, or 1. ... Kb6 2. Be3#. The underpromotion to a knight is necessary, for 1. d8=Q? is stalemate.

8. The try 1. Nb3 hoping for 1. ... d5? 2. Nd4# is refuted by 1. ... d6!, and there's no mate. Also 1. Bh3? expecting 1. ... Kd5 2. Bg2# has the flaw 1. ... d6!. The key is 1. Nb7, threatening 2. Qc4#. If 1. ... d5 2. Qa4#, or 1. ... Kb5 2. Bxd7, or 1. ... Kd5 2. Nb4#.

9. Here's another futile mission for Black's d-pawn. After 1. Rc5, Black is in zugzwang. If 1. ... d6 2. f5#, and 1. ... d5 allows 2. Rc6#. And 1. ... Kd6 is met by 2. Qe5#.

10. Black has only one piece, and White tempts it to move, at the Black king's peril. After 1. Re2, the move 1. ... Bxg1 allows 2. Re6#, and 1. ... Bxh6 allows 2. Ne8#. The f-pawn is no help, since 1. ... f4 is met by 2. Qg5#, and the king can't help itself: 1. ... Ke5 2. Qa1#, or 1. ... Ke7 2. Qg5#.

11. The wonderfully counterintuitive key to this frequently anthologized problem by the composing genius W. Shinkman is 1. Ba4, which threatens nothing and moves a strong piece almost off the board. Black is left to choose the manner of his own demise. If 1. ... d6 2. Nbc7#; 1. ... f6 2. Ndc7#; 1. ... f5 2. Qg8#; 1. ... Kxd5 2. Bb3#; 1. ... e4 2. Qxe4#.

12. Those two Black bishops on h1 and h2 look about to murder the White king ... but it's the Black king that gets killed. The key, 1. Rd8, threatens 2. Qe7#, and there's nothing Black can do to save his skin. If 1. ... b5 2. Qa5#. If 1. ... c5 2. Nb5#. If 1. ... Rd5 2. Rxc6#. If 1. ... Rc5 2. Rh7#. And if 1. ... Re5 or 1. ... Bd6, 2. Q(x)d6 ends it.

13. The art of threatening nothing is demonstrated by 1. Nf6. Black has only a few possible moves, but each allows White to mate him. If 1. ... Ne7 or 1. ... Nh6, then 2. Q(x)e7#. Or if 1. ... Nh~ then 2. N(x)g4#. If 1. ... Nxf6 2. f4#, or if if 1. ... Kxf6 2. Qg7#. If 1. ... d3 2. Qb2#.

14. The triple-purpose key, 1. Be8, controls the squares f7 and g6, frees the square d7 for the Ne5, and clears the way for the queen to get to d8. It also threatens 2. Nf3#. If 1. ... g6+ 2. Nf7#, or 1. ... g5+ 2. Nd7#, or 1. ... Be6 2. Qd8#, or 1. ... Ke7 2. Ng6#.

15. When it comes to surprising key moves, few can match 1. Nc1, putting a second piece en prise to a Black pawn, and this time allowing Black to capture while promoting. But each promotion leads to mate: 1. ... bxc1=Q/R 2. Qf3#, or 1. ... bxc1=B 2. Qf3# or 2. Nc3#, or 1. ... bxc1=N 2. Nc3#. If 1. ... Kxc1 2. Qh1#.

16. The Black bishop lurking on h1 is aimed directly at White's king in the opposite corner. Yet White has the nerve to open that diagonal with 1. Ng5, allowing a discovered check by Black's Ne4. But it's a vain hope: if 1. ... Nxd2+ or 1. ... Nxg5+ 2. Rd5#, or 1. ... Nxd6+ 2. Ndf3#. Else 2. Nxe4#.

17. The bishop wants to mate on d5 but the Black king can escape to c5. Thus 1. Ra5. If 1. ... Nc7 to cover d5, then 2. Bd7#. If 1. ... Nc5 or 1. ... Nb4 2. N(x)b4#.

18. After the brave 1. Rg7, the alignment of the Black queen and White king seems to promise Black ways to avoid mate, but no, White has the moves. If 1. ... exf5 2. Nf7#, or 1. ... e5+ 2. Ne6#. Black's attempt to find an escape square by 1. ... e3 or 1. ... Ke5 fails to 2. Qh2#, or 1. ... Kg3 2. Nxe4#, or 1. ... Ke3 2. Nh3#. Otherwise 2 Nf3#.

19. The powerful White queen is decisive after 1. Nc3, threatening 2. Nb5#. If 1. ... Qe2 2. Qh7#, or if 1. ... Qe8 2. Qxh2#. If 1. ... Bc6 2. Na6#. Otherwise 2 Nb5#.

20. The Black queen is pinned and can do nothing to prevent the various mates surrounding it. After the key, 1. Qc7, the immediate threat is 2. Qxc5#. If 1. ... Qxb5 2. Nxb5#, or if 1. ... Qd5+ 2. Nc6#. The escape attempt 1. ... Kd4 is squelched by 2. Qxc5#, as promised. Meanwhile, on the other side of the board, if 1. ... Nf6 (preparing ... Nd5), then 2. Nf5#. Or if 1. ... Nxf4 2. Bg7#. And if 1. ... e3+, reminding White that Black has a bishop on g2, then 2. Nb7#.

21. Here's a sweet little waiting move: 1. f3. All of Black's defenses are pawn moves: 1. ... cxd4 2. Qa2#, or 1. ... cxb4 2. Qb5#, or 1. ... c4 2. Qe4#, or 1. ... exf4 2. Qe6#, or 1. ... exd4 2. c4#, or 1. ... e4 2. fxe4#.

22. With one rook already en prise, White throws the other one into the fire with 1. Rf6, threatening 2. Rfxe6#. Black can't take either rook: if 1. ... Kxd6 2. Bf4#, or 1. ... Bxd6 2. Bc3#, or 1. ... Kxf6 2. Qxa1#.

23. With relatively few pieces on the board (a problem with at least eight but no more than twelve pieces is called a Meredith), B.G. Laws, a famous composer of long ago, puts everything to good use in this clear construction. The key is 1. Rd6, threatening 2. Qxd5#, and if now 1. ... Bxd6 2. Qg7#, or 1. ... Rc5/b5/a5/d3/d2/d1 2. Bh2#; or 1. ... Rxd6 2. Ng4#; or 1. ... Rd4 2. Re6#; or 1. ...Kd4 2. Qxd5#; or 1. ... Kxd6 2. Qc7#.

24. White offers his queen to two Black pieces in order to be able to play a discovered mate with either of his bishops: 1. Qc3, threatening 2. Qxe5#. The ingenious symmetrical consequences of the sacrifice are hard to see. If 1. ... bxc3 2. Ba3#, or 1. ... Rxc3 2. Bb1#. Stopping the mate with 1. ... Qxb2 allows 2. Bxc2#.

25. 1. Ng5 would be mate were it not for the Black king's escape to d5. The key, 1. Rd5, blocks that escape route and prepares the knight mate. If 1. ... Bxd5 or 1. ... Kf7 2. Ne5#, or 1. ... Kxd5 2. Nb6#. If 1. .,.. Bxd7 or 1. ... Nxe4 2. Qg8#. If 1. ... Nf7 2. Ndf6#.

26. The key, 1. Bd4, blocks the d-file so that White's rook can mate on d8, and also vacates the square g7 so that White can play 2. Ng7#. If 1. ... Ne6 or 1. ... Re7 2. R(x)e7#. On other moves, either 2. Rd8# or 2. Ng7# works.

27. There are many false trails here due to the exposed Black king and free-roaming White queen. The mission is accomplished, however, only by 1. Re3, threatening 2. Rxe5#. Black can try to defend with 1. ... Qxc4, but that takes the queen away from d7, so 2. Qd7#. If 1. ... Qd4, threating to take the Nc4, then 2. Qg8#. If 1. ... Qxe3 or Qc7, then 2. c7#. The defense 1. ... Qd6 allows 2. Ncb6#, or 1. ... e4 2. Qxe4#, or 1. ... Bxe3 2. Nc3#.

28. No discovery by the bishop here—the Rh1 is attacked by the Ba8—but that situation can change without warning. The key is 1. Qa6, threatening the pretty 2. Rd1#. If 1. ... Rb7+, blocking the a8-h1 diagonal, then 2. Bb6#, or 1. ... d5+ 2. Bc5#, or 1. ... Re4+ 2. Bd4#. Other tries are 1. ... e1=Q/R/N 2. Rf3#, or 1. ... e1=B 2. Re3/f3#, or Ke1 2. Qa1#.

29. Discoveries by the knight are premature due to Black ability to interpose his rook on d5, protected by the Bb3. To remove that defensive possibility, White has the clever key, 1. Qa4, threatening 2. Qg4#. If 1. ... Rxa4 2. Nc4#, or 1. ... Bxa4 2. Nb5#. Otherwise 2. Qg4#.

30. Again we see two Black bishops menacing the White king (see No. 12), but White pays them no heed. The key, 1. Nh4, threatens 2. Rh6#. If the Nd5 moves anywhere with check, then 2. Rb7# puts the pieces back in the box, except 1. ... Nc7+ 2. d5#, or 1. ... Ne7+ 2. Rg2#.

31. The mechanics of a problem are so much fun when the pieces get in each other's way. The key, 1. Bb5, threatening 2. Qc6# or 2. Qf5#, clears the second rank for White's rook, so if 1. ... axb5 2. Rc2#. If 1. ... gxf3 2. Rg5#. 1. ... g3 clears the short diagonal and allows 2. Qxh5#, and 1. ... Kxb5 is answered by 2. Qd5#.

32. A centralized king is not always a great idea. The Black king here is doubly threatened along the a1-h8 diagonal, so White calmly removes one of the attackers with 1. Qc1 and waits to see what Black will do. Not that it matters. If 1. ... exf6 or 1. ... Rxf6 2. Nc4#. If 1. ... exd6 2. Ne2# or 2. Ng4#. If 1. ... Rxd6 or 1. ... Kxf6 2. Ng4#. If 1. ... Kf4 2. Nxe6#. And if 1. ... Kxd6 2. Nb5#.

33. White's best piece needs to get out of its cage with 1. Qa7, threatening 2. Qa5#. The rest is clear: 1. ... Nd5 2. Rxa2#, or 1. ... Na4 2. Qe3# or 1. ... Nc4 2. Bc3#.

34. The positions of the pawns might suggest the solution: 1. c4. Black can't play either 1. ... bxc3 e.p. 2. Qxd4# or 1. ... dxc3 e.p. 2. Qd1#. As for other moves: 1. ... Rc8 2. Nxc8#; or 1. ... Rd8 2. Qxb4#; or 1. ... Nb7/c6/xc4/b3 2. Q(x)c6#.

35. Here's a clever clockwork mechanism. The key is 1. Nf4, and now: 1. ... g5 2. Rxf5#, or 1. ... Kxf4 2. Bd6#, or 1. ... Kxf6, Rg5/h5 2. Nd7#, or 1. ... Rxf6 2. Nxd3#, or 1. ... Rxf4 2 Re6#.

36. Some nice symmetry here with a couple of unlikely mating moves. The queen can't leave the b-file because of 1. ... bxc5; neither rook can move because the other rook or a knight would be left hanging; and the knights can't leave the protection of the rooks. That means a king move: the king can't go to the third or fifth rank because of 1. ... Rxa3 or 1. ... Rxa5. And 1. Kf4 is unsatisfactory because after 1. ... c6 White won't be able to play 2. Qf4#. After 1. Kh4, the defenses are: 1. ... c6 2. Qf4#; 1. ... d6/d5 2. Nc6#; 1. ... b5 2. Qxb5#; 1. ... Rxa5 2. R5c4#; 1. ... Rxa3 2. R3c4#; 1. ... Nb3/c2 2. N(x)c2#.

37. Set up the good old bishop discovery with 1. Re2! and Black is in zugzwang: 1. ... Ke5 2. Bd3#' or 1. ... Kd7 2. Bc6#; or 1. ... Kf7 2. Bxg6#; or 1. ... B~ 2. Qd5#; or, finally, 1. ... c6 2. Rxe7#.

38. An immediate discovery doesn't work; e.g., 1. Nc3+ Kxa6. Also wrong is 1. Qd7, threatening 2. Ndc7+, but 1. ... d1=Q provides a piece to interpose at d5. The key is 1. Qd3!, threatening 2. Nc3. If 1. ... Kxa6 2. Nd6#, or 1. ... Ka4 2. Qxa3#.

39. Again a bishop discovery fails, this time because of 1. ... Qxg8 (which is also the answer to 2. Rb8+). The winning idea is to get the Black queen off the g-file while also blocking its access to the 8th rank. Moving the rook from b6 adds the threat of Nb6#. But where to move the rook? If

1. Rc6 Qxc6+ (2. Nb6+ Qxb6#). If 1. Rd6 Qg1 (1. ... Qxd6 2. Bxd6#). If 1. Re6 Qxe6. But 1. Rf6! solves it, for if 1. ... Qg1 2. Bg3#, or 1. ... Qxf6 2. Bd6#.

40. The promotion 1. d8=Q looks strong but leads nowhere; Black's king escapes, depending on White's next move, to f6 or d6. The tempting 1. Qf3 threatens 2. Qf4# but fails to 1. ... c6 and there's no mate. But after 1. Qc2 the mate can't be stopped. If 1. ... Kf5 2. Kd4#, and if 1. ... Kd6 2. Qxc7#.

41. There are so many checking keys available—10 by the queen, three by the knights (some of them, admittedly, not worth a look)—that it would hardly seem necessary to look for something else. But in chess problems, as you know, things are seldom what they seem, and checking keys, as you also know, are generally frowned upon (a discovered check is still a check). The most unlikely move (which, in problems, is perversely the most likely) is 1. Rg6, which breaks the discovery possibility and threatens 2. Re6#. The defenses are: 1. ... Bd5 2. Qxc2#; 1. ... e5 2. N7d6#; 1. ... Kxf5+ 2. Rc6#; 1. ... Rxf5/g4+ 2. R(x)g4#; 1. ... Rh4/f3 2. Q(x)f3#; 1. ... Bd4 2. Ng3#.

42. Chess players like to say "the threat is stronger than the execution," although that axiom doesn't really make logical sense. What it's supposed to mean is that a strong threat forces the opponent to make concessions that are more unfavorable than if the threat were actually carried out. Here, for example, 1. Nd4 threatens 2. Rg4#. In avoidance of this threat, Black allows other mates, especially by the White queen. If 1. ... exd4 2. Qxd5#. If 1. ... Qxd4 2. Qxh7#. If 1. ... Kxd4 2. Qb4#. If 1. ... Bxd4 2. Qb1#. White's knight can be taken in four different ways, each leading to a different mate by the same piece.

43. Black's queen is pinned, which White exploits with 1. Rf3, clearing c3 to make 1. Nc3# possible. If Black breaks the pin with 1. ... Rd4, allowing the queen to protect c3, the rook blocks d4 and allows 2. Qe6#. If Black tries 1. ... Nd4, to break the pin and at same time prevent 2. Qe6#, the knight gives up its protection of e3 and allows 2. Re3#.

44. Black is almost in zugzwang already. The two knights are protecting the sensitive pawns on a6 and c5, and the king has only one move, to a5. Then Qxc5 would be mate were it not for the knight on a4. That thought leads

to 1. Ra1. Now 1. ... Ka5 allows 2. Qxc5#. Other moves by either knight allow 2. Rxa6# or 2. Rb7#, and if 1. ... a5 2. Rb7#.

45. The threats to White's king look worse than the threats to Black's, considering the Black battery along the h1-a8 diagonal. But with 1. Be7, threatening 2. Be6#, White forces Black to hamstring his own bishop. The defense 1. ... Rae4 blocks that diagonal and allows 2. Qf6#. The same goes for 1. ... Rge4 2. Qxg6#. If Black blocks the diagonal with a knight with 1. ... Nbd5 or 1. ... Ned5, then 2. Qe6#.

46. The Ne6 would like to mate on d4, but the knight would be blocking the d-file, allowing the Black king to escape to d7. So White first plays 1. Qg4, threatening 2. Nd4#. If 1. ... Kd5 2. Ng5#, or 1. ... Kb5 2. Nc7#, or 1. ... Kd7 2. Nxg7#.

47. The queen can't mate on the a3-f8 diagonal, so it switches to the other side with 1. Qa3, threatening 2. Qg3#. If 1. ... Rxa3 2. Nc4#. If 1. ... Nd~ 2. Nf3#. And if 1. ... gxh3 to stop the queen from going to g3, then 2. f4#.

48. After 1. Qd2, most defenses are refuted easily; for example: 1. ... Rxd3 2. Qxd3#; or 1. ... Qd7 2. Rxd7#, etc. The two most interesting mates are 1. ... Rc5 2. Nb6#, and 1. ... Rf1+ 2. Bb1#! (but not 2. Bxf1 Ke4).

49. The clearance move, 1. Rh5, threatens 2. Qc5# and causes havoc in the Black camp. If 1. Qa3/b4/d5 2. R(x)d5#. If 1. ... Qxc3 2. Qg4#, or 1. ... Qc4 Qh8#. Finally, if 1. ... Nd3 2. e3#.

50. Under the right circumstances, White will promote his e-pawn. But first he needs 1. Rbd5 to set up the mate threat 2. Rd6#. If 1. ... Nf6, enabling the king to escape to e5, then the fancy but necessary 2. exf8=N#. If 1. ... Bxg3 or 1. ... Rf6 2. e8=Q/R#. If 1. ... Bf6 2. Qg8#. And if 1. ... Bxe7 2. Qxe7#.

51. The straightforward 1. Re3 threatens 2 Qc4#. If 1. ... Bf5 or 1. ... Re5 2. R(x) e5#. If 1. ... Bxf7 2. Qxd7#. If 1. ... fxe3 2. Bg2#. If 1. ... Nd4 2. Bc4#. If 1. ... Nd2 2. Rd3#. And if 1. ... Rd4 2. Qa8#.

52. The bishop standing on f5 is not protecting that square, because it's standing on it. It's a common device in problems (and in chess play) to protect a square by withdrawing from it. By moving the bishop to c8, 1. Bc8, White enables his knight to move to g8, 2. Ng8#. If 1. ... Bd5 2. Nxd5#. If 1. ... cxd6, to give the

king a couple of escape squares, then 2. Qxd6#. If 1. ... c6, pinning the knight, 2. Qf3#, or if 1. ... c5 2. Qa1#.

53. White's knight allows itself to be captured in three different ways, each of which leads to mate. After 1. Ne3 the defense 1. ... Rxe3 is met by 2. d3#, or if 1. ... Bxe3 2. dxe3#, or if 1. ... dxe3 2. d4#. The escape attempt 1. ... Kf2 is answered by 2. Qf1#, and if 1. ... f2 2. Qd1#.

54. Here is one of those miraculous keys, 1. Be6, in which a White piece puts itself en prise to three different Black pieces, yet Black is helpless to prevent mate. If 1. ... Kxe6 2. d5#, or 1. ... fxe6 2. Rf8#, or 1. ... Qxe6 2. d5#. If 1. ... Qc5 2. dxc5#, or 1. ... Qe5 2. dxe5#. If 1. ... Qxd4 2. Bxd4#. If 1. ... Qa3 or 1. ... Qb8 2. Nd5#.

55. 1. Ne7+ would be mate were it not for the unprotected knight on d4. Protecting the knight by 1. Qb2, however, allows such defenses as 1. ... Bxf5 or 1. ... Nxd4, and protecting it by 1. Rc4 is foiled by 1. ... Rd3 (so that if 2. Qa8+ Bc6). The key is 1. Qa8, threatening 2. Rc5#. If 1. ... Nxd4 2. Ne7#, or if 1. ... Bxf5 2. Rc4#, or 1. ... Bxc6 2. Qxc6#.

56. This refreshingly clean composition is by the great Russian constructor L.K.A. Kubbel. The tempting 1. d4+ fails to 1. ... Kf4 2. Nd3+ Kg5, and after 1. Ne6+ Kf6 there's no mate. The key is 1. Rf6, threatening 2. Qd6#. If 1. ... Kd5 2. Nb3#, or 1. ... Kf4/d4, Qxf6+ 2. Ne6#, or 1. ... Kxf6 2. Ne4#.

57. The key to this rather intense problem is 1. Bc2, threatening 2. Qxe5#. If 1. ... Nfg4 2. Rf4#, or 1. ... Neg4 2. Rd3#, or 1. ... Nf5 2. Rg4#. If 1. ... Bxf3+ 2. Ndxf3#. White can't play 1. Bh7 because after 1. ... Qe4 or 1. ... Qf5 there's no mate.

58. With the White king in such an exposed position near the enemy queen, there's always the possibility of a queen check to spoil White's fun. White takes care of that danger with the sweeping key 1. Qf1. Black's queen remains pinned, and any move by the rook runs into 2. Qf4#. If 1. ... Qe3+ 2. Rxe3#, or 1. ... Qe2 2. R(Q)xe2#. If 1. ... Qxe1 2. Qxe1#. If 1. ... Nc7/g7/d6/f6 2. Q(x)f6#.

59. Sometimes it pays to be nice to your enemy. At the moment, the Black king has no flight squares, but there's no way to mate it where it stands. So White gives it a flight square: 1. Rc5! (blocking the queen's diagonal),

and now: 1. ... Kd4, Nf8/h8/e5/h4 2. R(x)e5#; 1. ... Ke3 2. Rc4#; 1. ... Rf5/xf6/g4/h4/f3/f2/f1 2. Qb4#.

60. The inner workings of this problem are hard to see because of the mutual pins. The key is 1. Bg6, threatening 2. d4#. To prevent that, Black can try 1. ... Ndb5, which unpins the White rook and allows 2. Re6#. The defense 1. ... Ncb5 also unpins the rook, allowing 2. Rc5#. The move 1. ... Ne6 unpins the White queen and allows 2. Qe4#.

61. If you've looked at the hint, you know that the key is a queen move, but to where? The queen is needed to protect the rook and keep the Black king from escaping, but neither 1. Qd7 Nb3 nor 1. Qc6+ bxc6 does the trick. And 1. Qf7+, 1. Qg6, and 1. Qh5 all give up the rook and allow the king's escape. But wait: after 1. Qh5 Kxb5 2. Bd3# is mate! If 1. ... Bxb5 then 2. ... Qf7# does the job. If 1. ... Bb3 2. Rc5#. If the Nc2 moves, 2. Rb4#. And if the Nc1 moves, 2. Qe2#.

62. Discovered checks by the bishop don't work because, of course, of 1. ... Rxe8. But if the Black rook were not on the 8th rank, then 2. Bxc7 would be mate. And if the knight on c7 should move, then 2. Bb8 would be mate. Both of those losing

Black moves come into play when White moves 1. Qa6, threatening 2. Rxe1#. Now if 1. ... Ne~ 2. Qd3#. If 1. ... f2 (to let the king escape to f3), then 2. Qe2#. If 1. ... b5, the queen swings over to the right and mates with 2. Qg6#.

63. One of the points of the key, 1. g7, is that the pawn move clears the square g6 for the knight to mate after 1. ... e6 2. Ng6#. Other defenses: 1. ... Bb5/b7/c8 2. Qa1#. If 1. ... Bxc4+ 2. Nxc4. If 1. ... Bc5/c7/b8 2. Q(x)c5#. If1. ... Nf5/h5/e2/f1/h1 2. R(x)f5#. If 1. ... Ng4/d3/h3/d1/h1 2. N(x)g4#

64. White's pawn has two possible captures, 1 dxc5 and 1. dxe5, both of which are answered by a knight recapture. Can either of those pawn captures be turned into mate? See what happened after 1. Rd2, making either pawn capture a discovered check. If 1. ... cxd4 or 1. ... c4 2. Qc6#. If 1. ... Ke4 2. dxc5#. If 1. ... exd4 or 1. ... Nf3+ 2. B(x)f3. If 1. ... e4 or 1. ... Ne4 2. Ne3#.

65. 1. f3 looks promising, cutting of the Black bishops' defense of the g-pawn and threatening 2. Qxg4#, but the bishop still defends the pawn with 1. ... Bxf3. A more surprising mate comes from two other directions: 1. Qe8, offering the queen to the Black queen and rook and threat-

ening 2. Qe7#. If 1. ... Qd8 or 1. ... Qxe8, mate comes on the h-file with 2. Rh2#. The same mate follows 1. ... Nc6, 1. ... Rb7, 1. ... d5, 1. ... e4, or 1. ... Ne4. If 1. ... Qb7 or 1. ... Nc8 2. Qxh8#. If 1. ... Qxg2+ 2. Nxg2#. If 1. ... Rf8/xe8/h5 2. R(x)h5#. Finally, if 1. ... Nf3 2. Rxg4#.

66. The key, 1. Qc8!, threatens 2. Qxc6#. If 1. ... Qa4/a5/c5/d6 2. Bf3#. Or if 1. ... Ne3 or Nc3 2. Bf3#. If 1. ... Nf6 2. Qe6#. And if 1. ... Qd3 (to be able to put the queen on d5 after the check) 2. cxd3#. Other White moves, such as 1. Qc7, allow the defense 1. ... Qa5, for now 2. Bf3+ is answered by 2. ... Kxf5 (the knight is unprotected).

67. The Nd4 could give mate at c6 if that move didn't cut off the Bb7's protection of the d-pawn (1. Nc6+? Kxd5). The key, 1. e4, makes that mate threat possible by taking over protection of the d-pawn. If 1. ... Bxd5 2. exd5#. If 1. ... Nxd4 2. Bxd6#. If 1. ... Kxd4 2. e5#. If 1. ... Rf5+ 2. exf5#. If 1. ... Rxf3+ 2. Nxf3#.

68. Black's looming ... d2 is no reason to fear moving the queen: after 1. Qe5 d2+, the final answer is 2. Nc3#, which also follows 1. ... Rxe5. If the Black knight moves, then 2. Qxe3#. Finally, the escape attempt 1. ... Kd2 is met by 2. Qb2#.

69. A bishop discovery doesn't work—yet!—because of … Nxh4. But after 1. Qf1, threatening 2. Qb1#, the knight has to move to give the king an escape square, and then the bishop discovery works.

70. First the Bg2 needs to protect the f-pawn to relieve the knight of that duty. Then, 1. Be4 threatens 2. Nxc4#. If 1. … Nxd6+ 2. Bd3#. If 1. … Ne5+ 2. Rd3#. If 1. … Nxe3+ 2. Nb5#. If 1. … Ke5 2. Nf7/c4#.

71. "Pinning and winning" is what chess players like to say when they can win a piece by pinning it. The pin has a different purpose here, but "pinning and winning" still applies The key, 1. Rb4, pins the Nc4 and thus threatens 2, Qe5#. If 1. … d4 2. Nd5#. If 1. … Rd4 2. Ng2#. If 1. … Be4 2. Qh6#. If 1. … Ne4 2. Qf5#.

72. After 1. Qf2, threatening 2. Qe2#, the Nd7 can't move (e.g. 1. … Nxe5) because of 2. Nc5#. The Nb6 can't go to d5 (preparing … Ne3) because of 2. Bf5#. 1. … Kxe5 exposes the king to the discovery 2. Bg8#, and 1. … Kd3 is met by 2. Bf5#. If 1. … Bd3 2. Qf4#.

73. This wide-open construction, with White's queen, both rooks, and both bishops working at maximum efficiency, appears to promise a forceful key, yet the answer is the most modest move possible: 1. d4. By protecting the squares c5 and e5, the pawn move relieves the Nd7 of those duties and allows it to threaten 2. Nb6#. Black defenses: 1. … Nxd7 2. Qe6#; 1. … Bxd4 2. Nf6#; 1. … Ra6/xd4 2. Nb4#; 1. … Rd3, Be4+ 2. Q(x)e4#; 1. … Bd3 2 Nc3#.

74. This rather complex position is unlocked by the modest 1. c4. First of all, the move frees the c2-square and threatens 2. Qc2#. If Black yields to the tempting 1. … bxc3 e.p.+, White mates with 2. Bb6#. If 1. … Bxe3 2. Qxe3#, or 1. … Bxc4# 2. Qxc4#. If 1. … Rxg2 (so that if 2. Qc2# Kxe3) 2. Bxf3#. Finally, if 1. … f1=N (to interpose at d2) 2. Re1#.

75. The Black king is frozen in place, but each of White's available moves lets it off the hook one way or another. For example, 1. Qg4+ N or Qe4. Or 1. Rc5+ Kb4. But 1. Qg8+ threatens 2. Qc8#, and mate cannot be avoided. All attempts at interposing something along the c-file fail. If 1. … Nb5 2. R5d4#, or 1. … Ne4 2. Rg5#, or 1. … Qf2 2. Rf5#. If 1. … Qxd5 2. Qxd5#, or 1. … Bxc3+ 2. R3d4#, or 1. … Bb4 2. Rc5#, or 1. … Bf2 2. Rxg3#.

76. White breaks his own pin of the Black queen temporarily, but this doesn't help Black at all. After 1. Rc5, the threat is 2. Rd5#. If 1. ... Qxc5 2. Nc4#, or 1. ... Qxf4 2. Ne4#, or 1. ... Qxb5 2. Ne4#, or 1. ... Kxc5 2. Nd3#, or 1. ... Qxd2+ 2. Qxd2#.

77. 1. Qh6 is a nice mate, but first the Re4 must be protected. And don't forget that nasty bishop lurking at a1. All in all, the key, 1. Rgg5, threatening 2. Qh6#, looks promising. The defense 1. ... h5 invites the rook back to g6. Almost any move by the Rc4 allows 2. B(x)c5#. If 1. ... Rc3 2. Re3#. If 1. ... Nd4 2. Re2#. Finally, if 1. ... Bxe5+ 2. Qxe5#.

78. The threat to Black's g-pawn is almost too good to be true, but mating at g7 is not a foregone conclusion. The king has to be let out of its cage to be mated. After the key, 1. Rf5, Black can choose among 1. ... Kh7 2. Rf8#, 1. ... Rh7 2. Rb8#, 1. ... B~ 2. Rxg7#, or 1. ... g6/g5 2. Bc4#.

79. White's queen is separated from its queenside forces by that little pawn on e5, which graciously gets out of the way with 1. e6, threatening 2. Qd4#. If 1. ... Be4 2. Qg5#, or 1. ... Bc4/xb3+/xe6+ 2. Qe5#, or 1. ... Bc6+/b7+/a8+ 2. Nxc5#, or 1. ... Ke4 2. Nd2#, or 1. ... f2 2. Re2#.

80. Take a break with this easy one. The slightly brutal key, 1. Bb6, directly threatens 2. Qxa7#. Black has only a couple of defenses: if 1. ... Kxb6 2. Qd6#, or 1. ... axb6 2. Qa8#. Now, wasn't that refreshing?

81. Incredibly, the knight throws itself into a bramble bush; it can be captured in no fewer than four different ways, each leading to mate on the next move. The key is 1 Nd6, threatening 2 Nb7#. If 1. ... cxd6 2. Bb6#. If 1. ... exd6 2. Rxc7#. If 1. ... Qxd6 2. Qc1#. If 1. ... Kxd6 2. Qxe7#.

82. The obvious 1. cxd4 is no good because of 1. ... Bxf7 and there's no mate. But Black is in zugzwang: any move is met by mate. If White could open the b-file, then Qb2 would be mate. That idea suggests 1. Nd8. Now if 1. ... Bxf7 or 1. ... Bd7 2. N(x)d7#. If 1. ... Bxc6 2. Nxc6#. If 1. ... Rxc5 2 Qb2#. If 1. ... Rd4 2. Bf4#. And if the Ng3 goes to f5, h5, c2, f1, or h1, then 2. R(x)f5#.

83. You can break a pin legally by moving the piece behind the pin, in this case the White king. The White Re4 is not only pinned, it also stands between the Black king and a discovered check by the White queen. The try 1. Kb5 fails to 1. ... Nxd2. The key is 1. Kc7. If then 1. ...Qh2+ 2. Re5#. There's some neat knight play: 1. ... Nxd2 2. Nc1#. If 1. ... Bxd2 2. Nc5#.

84. Pawn promotions are always tempting, but in this case 1. f8=Q leads to nothing: 1. ... Re3 (among other moves) stops any mate threat. Another possibility is 1. Qc6, threatening 2. Qe5#, but Black has the ready answer 1. ... Re3, and the a6-f1 diagonal is defended by the Na3. But the other light diagonal is vulnerable: the key, 1. Bh3, is a waiting move that has no answer: 1. ... Rxh3 2. Qxh3#; or 1. ... g5 2. Bf5#; or 1. ... N~ 2. Qc4#; or 1. ... R~ 2. Rf3#; or 1. ... dxc3 2. Qd7#.

85. The advance 1. e6+ is mighty tempting, but White is frustrated by the reply 1. ... Kd6. The key is 1. Qd3, threatening 2. Qc4#. To stop this, Black can try 1. ... Rd6+, but now comes 2. e6#. If 1. ... Rc6+ 2. Nde6#, or 1. ... Kxc5 2. Qb5#, or 1. ... Nxc5 2. ... c4#, or 1. ... Rxc5 2. Qf3#.

86. The ingenious key, 1. Qa6, threatening 2. Qxc4#, "pins" the Rc4 against the square d3, so that if the attacked rook moves, 2. Rd3 discovered check is mate. Other defenses: 1. ... Kd5/c5 2. Qxc4#, or 1. ... Bd3 2. Re5#, or 1. ... Bd5 2. Rc3#, or 1. ... Ne5 2. Qd6#.

87. With all that action on the d8-h4 diagonal, the key, 1. Bd7, discovers a mate threat to the Black bishop: 2. Qxg5#. Defending the bishop with 1. ... Rh5, or 1. ... Nh7, or 1. ... Ne4 runs into, respectively, 2. Nf5#, 2. Rh6#, or 2. Qf4#. If 1. ... Ng4 or 1. ... Rg4 2. hxg4#. If 1. ... Bf4 2. Rg4#, or if 1. ... Bh6 2. Qh5#.

88. The knights have all the fun after the key, 1. Nd5, threatens 2. Rc3#. If 1. ... Nb5 2. Nb6#. If 1. ... Nd7 2. Nfe3#. If 1. ... Nxd5 2. Nd6#. And if 1. ... Ne4 2. Nde3#.

89. The White queen sets the stage for interesting rook and bishop play. The key is 1. Qb7, threatening the discovered mate 2. Rc5#. If 1. ... gxh6, to provide for the king's escape to f5, the pawn deprives itself of the advance to g6 and thus allows 2. Qh7#. After that, the rooks and bishops play the major roles. If 1. ... Rxb6/d5 2 B(x)d5#, or if 1. ... Rxb4 2. Rc3#. 1. ... exf4 is met

by 2. Re6#. If 1. ... Bc5+ 2. Rd6#. Any other move by the Bd4 is answered by 2. Rc4#.

90. The Black king is vulnerable along the diagonal a2-g8 as well as by means of a discovered check along the a8-h1 diagonal. White's queen can't abandon the Rc6, so he first protects it with 1. Nfd4 (not 1. Nbd4 Kc4) to threaten 2. Qg8#. Black defenses: 1. ... Qxb5 2. Qd8#; 1. ... Qc3+ 2. Rxc3#; 1. ... Qxd4 2. Nc7#; 1. ... Qa7 2. e5#; 1. ... Qd6 2. exd6#; 1. ... Qe7 2. Rc7#; 1. ... Qf8 2. Rc8#; 1. ... Kc4 2 Qg8#.

91. One White move threatens two mates and at the same time blocks the two Black pieces that can defend against them. 1. Rg6 threatens both 2. b6# and 2. Bc5# (not 2. Bd6/e7/f8 Bd4). The rook move blocks the Black bishop so it can't take the Re4, and it blocks the Black rook so it can't take the White pawn when it gets to b6. Otherwise: 1. ... Bh6 2. bxa6#. 1. ... Bd4/e3/f2/g1, f6, Bxg6, Rh4 2. b6#. 1. ... b6 2.Bc3#. 1. ... axb5, Rxg6/h5 2. Bc5#.

92. A delicate balance with discovered mates all over the place. Every Black move is answered by mate, but every White move spoils it—every move but one: 1. Rc4. The Nf1 can't move because of 2. Q(x)g3#. If 1. ... Bxg7 2. Bxg7#; if 1. ... g3 2. Qf3#; if 1. ... Rd1/e2 2. N(x)e2#; if 1. ... Rxc1 2. Bc2#; 1. ... Re3 2. Bc3#; if 1. ... Rxe4 2. Bd4#; if 1. ... Ne3 2. Nd3#.

93. The pinned Black queen is attacked simultaneously by White's queen, bishop, and pawn, but instead of exploiting that situation, White's queen goes into hiding—but only temporarily. The key is 1. Qc1, threatening 2. Qa3#. If 1. ... Qd4 2. Nb7#, or 1. ... Qd3+ 2. Kxd3#, or 1. ... Qd2+ 2. Kxd2#, or 1. ... Qd1+ 2. Kxd1#, or 1. ... Qxe4+ 2. Nxe4#, or 1. ... Qc4+ 2. Nxc4#, or 1. ... Qxb3+ 2. Kxb3#.

94. The diagonal a2-g8, controlled by the White bishop-queen battery, is critical. The key is 1. Na5, smoothly threatening 2. Nb3#. Black has only a few defensive possibilities, mainly by trying to escape to the critical diagonal: 1. ... Be6 2. Qg7#; 1. ... e6 2. Qg4#; 1. ... Re6 2. Nf5#; 1. ... Rd5 2. Qxd5#; 1. ... Rxc1 2. Rad3#; 1. ... Rd3 2. Raxd3#; 1. ... Bd2 2. Rad3#; 1. ... Rd2 2. Bb2#.

95. The Black king has no moves; all White needs to do, it seems, is give check. But every check allows Black an escape. So it is necessary to wait for Black to unbalance the situation: 1. Qf2! poses no threat, but every Black answer falls into mate. If 1. ... Be5 2. Nxe5# or 1. ... Bb4 2. Ndxb4#. If 1. ... Bb8/c7/g3/h2 2. Ncb4#, or 1. ... Ba3/e7/f8 2. Ne5#. If 1. ... Na7/c7/d4/a3/c3 2. Q(x)d4#. Pawn promotions don't help, either: 1. ... e1=Q/R 2 Qc2#. Or 1. ... e1=B 2. Qc2/xf1#. Or 1. ... e1=N 2. Qxf1#. Finally, if 1. ... Ne3/g3/d2/h2 2. Q(x)e3#.

96. Another way to break a pin (see No. 83) is by interposing. Here we have mutual pins and cross-pins centered on the Qe5 with both queens en prise—a fantastic construction! It would be possible to play Rd1# if the Rd4 were not pinned. So let's break the pin with 1. Qb5. If 1. ... Rd4 2. Nf3# (the Black rook gives up f3). Or 1. ... Nf2, allowing 2. Rg1#. And if 1. ... Qxd5 or 1. ... Qe2 or 1. ... Qd4 or 1. ... Qxb2 or 1. ... Nge3 or 1. ... Nce3, then 2. R(x)e2#.

97. Why isn't 1. Ke5 discovered mate? Because Black's king escapes to g7, supposedly controlled by the Bb2. The key, 1. Bh8, swings the bishop to the other side of the king and cuts off that retreat. Now the threat is 2. Ke5#. Black's pieces are all bunched up in the corner, but he can still try to avert mate. If 1. ... Nf7 2. Bh7#. If 1. ... Nc6 2. Nf4#. If 1. ... Bd4 2. Kxd4#. The obvious 1. ... Bxd5+ runs into Kxd5#, The escape try 1. ... g4 allows 2. Kf4#, while 1. ... c6 2. Ne7# and 1. ... c5 2. Kxe3 take care of the other pawn moves. Finally, there is 1. ... Ng4/f3 2. K(x)f3#.

98. This cat-and-mouse game begins with 1. Qd8, threatening the discovery 2. Nfe6#. Black can try to defend by luring the White queen away from d8 by 1. ... Qxd2/Qb4/Qa5/Qc5/Qd3/Qf6, but White has the killer 2. Q(x)f6#. If 1. ... Qd4 2. Qxd4#, or 1. ... Qg7 2. Nxg6#. If 1. ... Kg7 or 1. ... Bf5+ 2. Nfe6#.

99. The d4-square is the intended mating spot after 1. Bb2, threatening 2. Qd4#. If 1. ... c5 2. Nb6#, or 1. ... e5 2. Nc3#. If 1. ... Nf7 2. Qg6#, or 1. ... Nf5 2. Nf6#. If 1. ... Rxd5+ 2. Bxd5#. If 1. ... b3 2. Qb1#. If 1. ... f2 2. Qh1#. Finally, if 1. ... Bc3/e3 2. Q(x)e3#. On the first move, if the Bd4 moves along the a1-h8 diagonal, 1. ... Be3 stops the mate, or if the bishop moves along the a7-f2 diagonal, then 1. ... Bc3 does it.

100. The queens and rooks battle it out in this puzzle. The key is 1. Re8, threatening 2. Qc8#. Black chases White's queen around but to no avail: 1. ... Qc3 2. Nxc3#; 1. ... Qa3 2. Nb4#; 1. ... Qxd5 2. Qxd5#; 1. ... Qe3/c4/b5 2. Ng(x)e3#' 1. ... Qg3+ 2. Nf4#; 1. ... Qa6+ 2. Nb6#; 1. ... Qe4 2. Ne7#. Finally, if 1. ... Rg7 2. Nh6#.

101. The queen needs to go to f4 to give mate, but that would leave the Nd5 unprotected. So the king takes charge with 1. Kc5, threatening 2. Qf4#. If 1. ... Nc~+ 2.Bxc2#, or 1. ... Ne5+ 2. Nc3#, or 1. ... e5 2. Nf6#.

102. There are so many tempting moves: g3+, fxe3+, Nd~+, etc., that the key, 1. Ka5, comes as a real surprise. By unpinning the king, White threatens 2. Ne2#. If 1. ... Qxf2 2. Nf5#, or 1. ... Qxe5+ 2. Nb5#. If 1. ... Rxd4 2. Nd3#. If 1. ... Qxd4 2. Rxd4#.

103. The queen wants to mate on d5 but is unable at the moment because White does not control d5. The key, 1. c4, solves that problem and threatens 2. Qd5#, but it also frees Black's queen to defend by going to e4. But that's not all that's going on. If 1. ... Be4 2. Qxg1#. If 1. ... Rc5 2. Bc3#. If 1. ... Rxc4 2. Nb3#. If 1. ... e4 2. Qg7#. If 1. ... Re4 2. Nf3#. If 1. ... Nxc4 2. Nxc6#. If 1. ... Qe4 2. Qxb2#.

104. Don't be distracted by the aggressive pawns on g7 and h7. The knight on e5, after 1. Bd4, is the focus of four different lines and threatens to mate in all directions. This rich modern masterpiece is a "knight-wheel" construction: the threats are: Nexc4#, Nf3#, Ng4#, and Nxc6#. Black's defenses are met thus: 1. ... Kd5 2. Nf3#; 1. ... Kxd6 2. Nxc4#; 1. ... Ke7 2. Nxc6#; 1. ... cxd4 2. Ng4#; 1. ... Kf6 2. Nxd7#; 1. ... Rxd3 2. Nxd3#; 1. ... Nxf7 2. Nexf7#; 1. ... Nxg6 2. Nxg6#. Also, if 1. ... Rxb3 2. Nexc4#.

105. The key, 1. Kf5, accomplished several things at once: it threatens 2. Bxc5#, unpins the Ne4, opens the diagonal a2-g8 for the queen, etc. It also allows Black to check the king in several ways but to no avail. If 1. ... Bd4+ 2. Be5#; 1. ... Be3+ 2. Nc5#; 1. ... Bxd6+ 2. Nb5#; 1. ... Rf1+ 2. Nf2#; 1. ... Rd1 2. Nd2#; 1. ... Nd7 2. Qd5#; 1. ... Nc7 2. Qxc7#.

106. Another ingenious Comins Mansfield composition. Despite all the heavy artillery on the board, the key is the modest 1. c3, threatening 2. Qxd4#. After 1. ... Bxc3, Black may be shocked to see 2. d3#. If 1. ... Bc5 2. Qd3#. If 1. ... Be5 2. Bxe6#. Black's knight can put in an appearance with 1. ... Nd5 but his act is canceled by 2. Qxc6#, or if 1. ... Ne2 2. Nxe3#. The reasonable 1. ... Bd5 or 1. ... Rd5 blocks d5 but allows 2. Qb4#.

107. White pays Black the courtesy of releasing the Ne3 from the pin with 1. Bb4. But it's a Greek gift: after 1. ... cxb6 2. Bd6# is mate, and that same mate greets 1... B~. If 1. ... Ng7/f6/g3 2. Q(x)g3#. If 1. ... Ke5 2. Qxe3#. If 1. ... Nd5/g4/g2/d1/f1 2. Qd4#. Finally, if 1. ... Nf5 2. Ng6#.

108. If White can induce the Black knights to move, he will be able to mate at d5 or f5. The first step in this plan is 1. g3, threatening 2. gxf4#. If Black defends with 1. ... Ne6 2. Rf5#. If 1. ... Bxd3+ 2. Nxd3#. If 1. Nde2 2. Qd5#. The obvious 1. ... fxg3 is met by 2. f4#. And if 1. ... Nce2 2. Qf5#.

109. The position looks very dense, but the fact is that Black, with all those pieces on the board, has only a few moves at his disposal. So when White plays 1. Qc1, threatening 2. Qe3#, Black is hard pressed to defend. If 1. ... Re4 2. Rd5#, or 1. ... Rf5 2. Ne6#. If 1. ... Rg4 2. Nef5#, or 1. ... Rf3 2. Re4#. If 1. ... Nd3 2. Rxc4#, or 1. ... Nc2 2. Qd2#.

110. In this clear-cut construction by the great Arnaldo Ellerman, White's key, 1. Qb2, threatens the sweeping 2. Qh8# or 2. Qg7#. Black's troubles extend to the g-file, too, as we shall see. If 1. ... c3 2. Bf4#, or 1. ... Rc3 2. Qb8#. If 1. ... Rxg3+ 2. Rxg3#, or 1. ... Rxb2 2. Bf2#. And if 1. ... Nc3 2. Be1#

111. The pin on Black's queen prevents the queen from participating in the defense. Black's knight has annoying discovered check possibilities after the 1. Nf6, threatening 2. Qd5#, but the checks are futile, however: if 1. ... N~+ 2. Bc4#, or 1. ... Nc6+ 2. Nc4#, or 1. ... Nxe6# 2. d4#, or 1. ... Nf5# 2. Qe4#.

112. This is a zugzwang problem, which means that any Black move is fatal. The key, 1. Ra1, prevents the Black king from escaping to the a-file. If 1. ... Kb4 2. Rd4#. If 1. ... Rc6+ 2. Qxc6#. If 1. ... Rxd5 2. Qxd5#. If 1. ... Rc8 2. Qxb5#. If 1. ... Nd4 2. Rxc5#. Finally, if 1. ... N~ 2. Qb3#.

113. Black's only escape is Kxg6, so White cuts it off with 1. Bc1, threatening 2. Qf4#. Black can try to interfere with White's threat with 1. ... Ne5 2. Ne7#, or 1. ... Be3 2. Bb1#, or 1. ... Be5 2. Qxd7#, or 1. ... Re4 2. Rg5#, or 1. ... Re5 2. Qf8#.

114. Black's king is vulnerable from many directions after 1. Qb1, threatening 2. Nd3#. The obvious defense 1. ... Qxa6 fails to 2. Nxa6#, and 1. ... axb4 fails to 2. Qxb4#. Now that the queen has left e4, the defense 1. ... Bd4 runs into 2. Ne4#. If 1. ... Rb2/d2 2. Rxa5#. If 1. ... Nb2 2. Qxg1#. Finally, if 1. ... d5, from out of nowhere comes 2. Bf8#.

115. In order to expose Black's sensitive squares, White moves his bishop out of the way with 1. Bf6 (any other bishop move is answered, ingeniously, by 1. ... Bd6, bring the Black rooks into play and staving off the mate), threatening 2. Rc5#. If 1. ... Qb6 or 1. ... Qc8 2. N(x)b6#. If 1. ... Qc6 2. Rd4#, or 1. ... Qd6 2. Qe4#, or 1. ... Qe6 2. Qc5#, or 1. ... Qxf6 2. Nxf6#. Eliminating the threatening rook doesn't help: if 1. ... bxc4 or 1. ... Nxc4 2. Bxf3#. If 1. ... Be5 2. Qxe5#. Finally, if 1. ... Bd6 2. Qf7#.

116. The king, all alone in the center of the board, is the target of many threats, primarily 1. Qf8, threatening 2. Bb2#. If 1. ... Na2 2. Qc5#, or 1. ... Nd3 2. Re4#, or 1. ... Nc6 2. Rb5#, or 1. ... Nd5 2. Re6#. If 1. ... Bf5 2. Qxg7#.

117. White has the good idea of getting the king off the line of Black's rook with 1. Kg3, threatening 2. Qf1#, but it puts the king in the direct range of Black's Bb8. If 1. ... cxb6+ 2. Nf4#, or if 1. ... c6+ 2. Ndc7#. Black's other bishop can move, too, but futilely. If 1. ... Bc6/a6/c8 2. Nd6# or if 1. ... Bxd5 2. Qxd5#. Finally, if 1. ... d3 2. Qf4#.

118. Among the characteristics of many 19th-century compositions was a bishop in a corner on an open diagonal. This suggested the possibility of the bishop's longest move, all the way to the opposite corner, a sort of "feat." In this case, the key is the provocative 1. Ba1, a waiting move that threatens nothing but leaves Black in zugzwang. If 1. ... Kf3/xf5 2. Qxd5#. If 1. ... Kd3, 1. ... f3, 1. ... Nxf5/e2/f1/h1 2. Qb1#. That the bishop move only to a1 forces mate is shown by the following unsuccessful alternatives: 1. Bg7 Kxf5; 1. Bf6 Kxf5; 1. Be5 Kxe5; 1. Bd4 Kxd4; 1. Bc3 Kd3; 1. Bb2 Kd3; 1. Bb2 Kd3 (among other moves).

119. The action takes place on the b1-h7 diagonal, where the White queen and rook are both pinned against the king by the Black bishop on c2. But the bishop is itself pinned. How can White get out of both pins in only two moves and also give mate? The answer is 1. Rd8, threatening 2. Qd3#, breaking the pin on the rook and ignoring the pin on the queen. If instead 1. Re3/f3, then 1. ... Kd4 and there's no mate. Or 1. Rd5 Qc3, or 1. Rd6 b4, or 1. Rd7 Re4. Black defense tries are: 1. ... Qc3 2. Na3#; 1. ... e4 2. Qd5#; 1. ... Nge4 2. Qe6#; 1. ... Re4 2. Qc8#; 1. ... Rd4 2. Rc8#; 1. ... Nde4 2. Qf1#.

120. One little move, 1. b6, blocks the action of two pieces that are preventing mate, the Black bishop on the a7-g1 diagonal, and the Black rook on the sixth rank. The two threats were 2. Nxf6# and 2. Nf2#. After 1. ... Bxb6 White still has 1. Nxf6#. Other defenses: 1. ... Rf7 2. Qxe5# or Nf2#; 1. ... Re6, Rxb6 2. Nf2#; 1. ... Ne8/g8/d7/xh5 2. Qf5#/e3#, Nf2#; 1. ... Nd5 2. Qf5#, Nf2#; 1. ... Nxg4 2. Qf5#; 1. ... Bxg2 2. Qf5#/e3#, Nxf6#; 1. ... Bxg4 2. Qe3#; 1. ... Nd3 2, Nxf6#, gxf3#.

121. The only move that works is 1. Qb1, threatening 2. Qe4#. (But not 1. N~+ Kxd5.) If now 1. ... Rf4, the queen stretches its muscles with 2. Qb8#. Or if 1. ... Rxf3 or cxd5 2. Ng4#. If 1. ... g5 2. Qa1#, and if 1. ... Ke6 2. Qf5#.

122. The pinned queen obviously can't move, but the pin can be lifted another way: 1. Kh5 even though now the queen can be captured by the rook, 1. ... Rxg3. But the cost to Black is 2. Nxg3#. Other tries: 1. ... Kxf5 2. Qf4#; 1. ... d2 2. Bc2#; 1. ... e2 2. Qxd3#; 1. ... Rxf1, Bg2 2. Qg4#; 1. ... Rg2, Bf3 2. Q(x)f3#.

123. Several Black pieces are currently under attack, but only one can be doubly attacked with mate added: the Nc6. The key is 1. Qa6, threatening 2. Qxc6#. All defenses fail: 1. ... Nb8/d8/xa7/a5 2. Rh5#; or 1. ... Ne7 2. Qd6#; or 1. ... Ne5 2. Nf6#; or 1. ... Ncd4, Rxb5, Ned4 2. Be4#; or 1. ... Rc4 2. bxc4#.

124. Problem composers love discovered checks, usually as the mating second move. Here's another one, after the key, 1. Nd4, which protects the c-pawn and allows the bishop to play 2. Bf5#. If 1. ... Qxe4+ 2. Bg4#. If 1. ... Nxe4 2. Be6#. If 1. ... Nxd4 2. Nc3#. And if 1. ... Bxc6 3. Bxc6#.

125. The most unlikely move on the board, 1. Ke5, threatens an unlikely discovered mate, 2. Kd4#. If 1. ... Qxf6+, the king snaps back with 2. Kxf6#. If 1. ...Rxe6+ 2. Kxe6#. If 1. ... Qxg6 2. Qxg6#. If 1. ... Bxf4, the king reacts again with 2. Kxf4# or if 1. ... Rxe4+ 2. Ke4#. The defense 1. ... Ne3 abandons the Bg3 to 2. Nxg3#. If 1. ... Bf2 2. Rf5#. If 1. ... Rc8/b8/a8 2. Bg4#. Lastly, if 1. ... Qd7/c7/b7/a7 2. Qf5#.

ABOUT THE AUTHOR

BURT HOCHBERG is the author of *Title Chess: The 1972 U.S. Chess Championship* (1972), *Winning With Chess Psychology* (with Pal Benko, 1991), *The 64-Square Looking Glass: The Great Game of Chess in World Literature* (1993), *Mensa Guide to Chess* (2003), *Sit & Solve Chess Problems* (2004), and *Outrageous Chess Problems* (2005). He was the editor-in-chief of *Chess Life* magazine for 13 years, senior editor (now editor emeritus) of *Games* magazine, Executive Director of the Manhattan Chess Club, Executive Editor of R.H.M. Press, and the author of the major articles on chess and electronic games for the Microsoft Encarta Encyclopedia. He received the "Outstanding Career Achievement" award by the U.S. Chess Federation and the Fred Cramer award as "Best Chess Book Editor" (both 1996). He has been a columnist for ChessCafe.com, and his articles have been anthologized in various journals. In 2004 he was a primary inductee to the new Gallery of Distinguished Chess Journalists.

ALSO AVAILABLE

Outrageous Chess Problems
Sterling ISBN 978-1-4027-1909-7